A Change of Plans

by Carol Peske illustrated by Shane McGowan

Scott Foresman
is an imprint of

Glenview, Illinois • Boston, Massachusetts • Mesa, Arizona
Shoreview, Minnesota • Upper Saddle River, New Jersey

Illustrations
Shane McGowan

Photographs
Every effort has been made to secure permission and provide appropriate credit for photographic material. The publisher deeply regrets any omission and pledges to correct errors called to its attention in subsequent editions.

Unless otherwise acknowledged, all photographs are the property of Pearson Education, Inc.

Photo locators denoted as follows: Top (T), Center (C), Bottom (B), Left (L), Right (R), Background (Bkgd).

12 (CL) ©Corbis Premium RF/Alamy, (L) ©Burke/Triolo Productions/Jupiter Images, (BC) Index Open

ISBN 13: 978-0-328-39315-2
ISBN 10: 0-328-39315-0

1 2 3 4 5 6 7 8 9 10 V010 17 16 15 14 13 12 11 10 09 08

Mark's family was planning a picnic. They planned to meet Nana at the park the next day.

"What are we taking with us tomorrow?" asked Dad.

"Here are a few things for sports," said Mark.

"Here is a blanket we can bring," said Mom.

"We can pack food tomorrow," said Dad.

Mom started to read the paper. "Oh, no," Mom said. "I'm afraid it will rain tomorrow."

"Oh, no!" said Mark.

"How can we have our picnic?" asked Jen.

It did rain the next day.

"It's time to go," Dad said.

"How can we have our picnic?" asked Jen again.

"You'll see," said Mom.

The family got in the car. Soon they stopped at Nana's house.

Mark and Jen went inside the house. Nana had set up a picnic! There was food sitting on the floor.

"You don't need a nice day for a picnic," Nana said. "You just need some food and some fun!"

Why the Earth Needs Rain

Rain brings water to the earth. People must have water to live. Most plants and animals need water too. What happens when there is no rain in a place for a long time? Ponds and streams dry up. Plants may turn brown and die. Many animals cannot survive. People cannot grow enough food. The earth becomes very dry. There may not be enough water to drink. Rain is very important.